Three Cheers for Poetry

- ASHOK SAWHNY -

An environmentally friendly book printed and bound in England by
www.printondemand-worldwide.com

This book is made entirely of chain-of-custody materials

www.fast-print.net/store.php

THREE CHEERS FOR POETRY

Copyright © Ashok Sawhny 2014

All rights reserved

No part of this book may be reproduced in any form by photocopying or any electronic or mechanical means, including information storage or retrieval systems, without permission in writing from both the copyright owner and the publisher of the book.

The right of Ashok Sawhny to be identified as the author of this work has been asserted by him in accordance with the Copyright, Designs and Patents Act 1988 and any subsequent amendments thereto.

A catalogue record for this book is available from the British Library

ISBN 978-178456-011-9

First published 2014 by
FASTPRINT PUBLISHING
Peterborough, England.

List of the Poems

1.
Three Cheers For Poetry

From prose did I a poem become
And it all happened one night,
No, it wasn't vodka nor was it rum,
That gave a blind man sight.

From the dullness of the written word,
Did melody come alive,
The heart a little fluttering bird,
And the brain began to jive.

I felt I could, at once, sing,
Pitter-patter through the veins,
Music that the clouds bring,
To ease my earthly pains.

And thus was born the poet in me,
The one who rejoices in verse,
And like the rhythm of the sea,
Rises and falls, for better or worse.

We all know what prosaic means,
And what life, less music, would be,
Those unromantic, dull, scenes,
Where plainness is all you see.

Thus poetry beats prose any day,
Cos poets speak from the heart,
So listen to what they have to say,
For there's no better place to start.

Three cheers then for Poetry,
And may words continue to dance,
I hope you too, dear reader, will,
Turn poet by happenstance.

2.
The Little Wave

One of trillions that an ocean makes,
I am that little wave,
And but for me there'd be no sea,
But does anyone about me rave?

I'm generally quiet and peaceful,
When daylight hits the shore,
For the sun does little to excite me,
While the moon does a whole lot more.

The gentle breeze and I,
We get along well together,
Like a house on fire, proverbially,
Like birds of similar feather.

I rock with the breeze and the breeze with me,
And together we make merry,
We try to be gentle as gentle can be,
When you, O reader, are in a ferry.

I know, I can scare you, perhaps,
With my ferocious demeanour,
But then you must forgive me, please,
Cos then I am no wave, O Traveller,

For I am then the angry ocean,
And in the storm I'm frightened too,
Cos I know I might never return,
To an ocean that's silent and blue.

For waves like me that batter the shore,
Could get swallowed by the patient sand,
And for ever become part of history,
And merge with arid land.

So think of me and kindly,
As I lap the shore today,
Remember, I'm your little wave,
And that's all I have to say.

3.
The Beauty Of Silence

Not a word said but all understood
For the eyes in silence spake,
Feelings emanating from the heart.
A language of their own make.

The ocean's calm and majestic
When waters run still and deep,
Journeys to the land of dreams for all,
Only when we go to sleep.

How will we ever find ourselves,
In the blabber and tumult around,
Only silence it is that will ensure,
That the self within is found.

Divinity is there in silence
And only there will you ever find,
The spirit, the soul, the essence of life,
Tranquillity and peace of mind.

4.
A Smoker's Lament

They drifted away into the skies,
And slowly from sight too,
Those lovely little circles I made,
When smoke I did and rings blew.

That pursing of lips was all I did,
Then gently formed those rings,
O what pleasure, what ecstasy,
That memory to the mind brings.

Four scores a day and rings aplenty,
But the rings in the dark were a treat,
For to lie on the back and reach for the stars,
With those rings was no mean feat.

On a starlit night with a 'ciggie' alight,
Was as close to heaven as I could be,
Every 'puffer' knows and all too well,
That feeling divine, you see.

Alas! Not for me those rings any more,
But miss them I do and miss them for sure.

5.
If All My Dreams Were Realised

If all my dreams were realised,
And if that were ever to happen,
What would I do I sometimes wonder,
Go back to nursery rhymes?

Perhaps the place to start again,
The climb to the top with Jack and Jill,
The hill I may have just descended,
When the last of my dreams has finally ended.

Cos there's no way up from the pinnacle,
When you've reached the very top,
You can touch the clouds, reach for stars,
But the nothingness around you jars.

So keep some hopes and dreams alive,
For that's all the wealth you have,
And chase them while you possibly can,
And enjoy the race you run and ran.

6.
Will I Ever This World Miss?

Will I ever this world miss,
And will the world miss me?
Answers to these questions alone,
Determine vision and how we see

The centrality of our lives,
To the world as we envision it,
And our places in the sun,
Both brightly and dimly lit.

I wonder if they ask themselves
What after me?
The tree, the flower and all that lives,
Or simply accept destiny.

In the carving out of destiny,
Have we not our ways lost?
Materially progressed, yes,
But values forgotten at great cost.

7.
What Is Happiness?

A happy mind is always joyful,
But sadly that isn't true,
For who has ever a rainbow seen,
Without a tearful sky, have you?

Then tell me if you will Ashok,
And tell me with finesse,
Is it fulfilment of desire or need,
What is happiness?

Is it things to collect
And memories to keep?
Midst the weariness of the body,
And the wonderment of sleep?

If happy times mean happiness,
Then what of days when you're sad?
When life does a burden seem,
And living doesn't make you glad.

So don't pretend to happiness,
When it's a heavy heart you carry,
Go shed some tears and lighten the load,
Why wait, why tarry?

Happiness, friend, is a state of mind,
And nothing more than that,
Remind yourself to happy stay,
And never wait for another day.

For it's up to you
And that is true!

8.
What Is Heaven And Where Is It?

What is heaven and where is it?
And where does it really lie?
Somewhere in the heart of Man,
Or somewhere in the sky?

These questions apply to hell too,
Is it truth or lie?
To keep you on the straight and narrow,
Invention on the sly?

Paradise is where you are,
And so the infernal fire,
Look within, not up, O Man,
Commands the heavenly Crier.

Heaven and hell, war and peace,
In the heart of Man rest,
As the journey of life puts each one,
Through a long and arduous test,

For us, through whatever means, to find
Ourselves, and attain peace of mind.

9.
The Falsity Of Hope

Keep hope alive is what is said,
How else are you going to live?
But to live on hope and hope alone,
Is to tie yourself to a stone,

That will drag you down,
To the bottom of the sea,
Cos within hope lies,
The seed of falsity.

For if you were to nothing expect,
Hope wouldn't let you down,
You'd be okay in tatters too maybe,
Not envy another's gown,

If instead you believe in destiny,
Then irrelevant would be 'hope'
You would pray to God within you,
And not to Man or Pope.

Expectation comes from hope,
Life's an opera, at times like a soap.

10.
Stars Shine When The Sky Is Dark

Stars shine when the sky is dark,
True beauty does in wilderness lie,
What's more poignant tell me, Ashok,
Than dew-like tears and a heartfelt cry.

In randomness does profundity lie,
Unchained, unrestrained and free,
And only when you shut your eyes,
Does the mind's eye begin to see?

The bud must for ever die,
For the flower to fully bloom,
Happiness is the natural state,
With occasional bouts of gloom.

Trees do the sunlight block,
Thank God they give us shade,
And when days begin to take their toll,
The night comes to our aid.

Good and bad are just both times,
And no more than simply that,
There is a balm for every ache,
In the form of a prayer and a mat.

11.
The Truth About Darkness

Everything does from darkness spring,
The sun and enlightenment too,
You plant the seed in a heap of mud,
Then look at the flower that looks at you.

There'd be no beauty without night
No stars, no moon would ever shine,
No sunsets nor ethereal dawn,
What then would you call divine?

No lamps would ever dot the hills,
No waves light up the seas,
Cos they would miss the beautiful moon,
And there'd be no calming breeze.

Let's not forget the start of Man,
Let's not forget the womb,
And when it's all done and dusted,
Lies a waiting tomb.

And the cycle of life thus goes on,
From dawn to dusk to night,
And as we dream through the slumber,
We wake up to the eastern light.

And then there is the mind's eye,
That only in the dark can see,
And reveals to you the contours of
Both life and destiny.

And that is the truth that gives us insight,
That darkness it is that leads to light.

12.
Those Times Were Nice

Those times were nice,
When we got from place to place,
Across the seas
At a relaxed, leisurely pace.

When time had meaning,
And we had time for it,
To gaze at the stars,
All beautifully lit.

And time for ourselves,
Was always there,
To do what we liked,
Even walk on air.

And never did we,
Have to go look for time,
Cos life was much more
Than dollars and dime.

The art of writing
Is now a chore,
And letters are alphabets,
Envelopes no more.

O, what will happen to postage stamps,
Cos lick we do now others' shoes,
The world small, so 'glocal' now,
But the lack of time, a ready excuse.

It's all GDP and technology,
Apples mean different things today,
You can't eat them, that's for sure,
Life has found another way

To destroy itself
By the numbers game,
Simplicity lost,
In the quest for fame.

People breathed and died the same,
As they do today,
But while they lived,
They lived another way,
Thank God.

13.
O, How We Forget And So Easily

O, how we forget and so easily,
That the end is still the same,
Give or take some years few,
And that's averages to blame.

Values lost, institutions destroyed,
And solutions then sought,
By a society that now believes,
That everything can be bought.

If deterrence was meant to deterrent be,
Then why would anyone choose hell,
And not do things that would have us ringing,
A glorious heaven's bell?

Cos the human being is no saint on earth,
And evil resides in all,
And the only way is to values teach,
To prevent the angel from a fall.

Screaming, shouting, TV anchors
Politicos of all hues,
Isn't it strange that nothing nice,
Ever makes the news.

Does it not tell you, please reflect,
How base is human nature,
The only thing that makes us smile,
Is now just caricature.

Good news is no news,
Is different from the times of old,
When no news was considered good,
And rubbish not sold as gold.

Voices in the wilderness,
Are voices nevertheless,
They simply say it bluntly,
Maybe lack finesse,
But don't you ever
Get them wrong.

14.
Is It Rose Or Is It Daisy?

Is it rose or is it daisy?
Is it lake or pond for you?
Is it rain or clear blue skies?
Verdant grass or morning dew?

Snow-capped peaks and icy glaciers,
Or warmer climes and tanning too,
What is it that you fancy?
A luxury liner or canoe?

Is it maths that you like,
Or is it rocket science for you?
Would you rather captain be,
Or be a member of the crew?

Different people, different views,
So learn we must to tolerate,
For only then can we live happily,
And make living truly great.

What God you pray to is up to you,
And if you don't that is your choice,
Respect we must what another says,
Cos each has an equal-weighted voice.

Who is right and who wrong?
These battles rage for long.
Speak your mind don't bottle it up,
For it may be your swansong.

To each his own was truly said,
Cos each of us is unique,
So why not learn to lavish praise,
And shun worthless critique.

15.
I Live The Day As It Passes By

I live the day as it passes by
Drawing to its close,
And as the sun does duly set
To light another's world,
I slip into the world of dreams,
The world that no one knows.

To be alone and with myself
The natural state of all
Who journey through this pilgrimage
Called Life,
Till summoned by the bugle,
The final call.

And as the hours go racing by
Through a deeply darkened day,
Some dreams I choose to dream about,
And some,
Surreptitiously,
Find their way.

The weary mind and body both,
In the night an ally find,
To lean on, to burden share,
To sleep through
Sans nightmare,
Peace, peace of a different kind.

Until the dawn of another day,
Another rise of the sun,
Until the days and nights too,
Are for me,
One day, or night,
Done.

And in the midst of night and day,
This chequerboard of Time,
There live,
The king, the queen, the knave and I,
Pawns at work,
And play.

Until then will I but soldier on
Walking to my beat,
For no other do I listen to,
Cos it's my life,
And so,
My treat.

But another will I never hurt,
Cos we all are much the same
Bits of gold in each,
And also bits of dirt.

16.
Whoever With Time Played

Whoever with time played
Was slowly put to rest,
Whoever with time stayed
Served time and self, best.

Your Time is just you,
And what you daily do,
Keep heaven and happiness close,
Or visit hell too.

Smile, don't frown at vicissitudes
And you will understand,
Life is a choir, an orchestra,
With many voices and a discordant band.

Each to a different drummer walks,
And croons to notes his own,
Pulsating rhythms that come from the heart,
Remember,
You will reap only that which you've sown.

17.
An Eye For An Eye

An eye for an eye,
Will leave us all blind,
And in time to come,
Annihilate mankind.

But such are the values,
Of the world today,
Where both sanity and wisdom,
Have lost their way,

That peace is a subject,
That needs to be taught,
O what a travesty,
In what web are we caught?

Are we too far gone,
In this world, Ashok,
Are we watching a play,
Called 'dagger and cloak'?

Where villains and heroes,
Are all destined to fall,
And the future of mankind
Too close to call.

18.
What's Outside Of You, O Ashok

What's outside of you, O Ashok,
Not much, friends, if you really want to know,
Cos we're all a world unto ourselves,
And what's beyond is mostly show.

Why then do we so empty feel
And crave for another, at times?
Cos you haven't befriended yourself, my friend,
And forgotten the beauty of rhymes.

You've lost the child in you somewhere,
In your quest for the world of men,
Where power and glory and ego is all,
And truth multiplied by ten.

See how happy the child is
All by itself and its toy,
Bat and ball or just a doll,
No matter girl or boy.

Lucky the person who understands,
The beauty of being alone,
You can lonely be in a multitude,
And happy on a solitary stone.

Cos the world derives its existence from you,
And not the other way round,
Why haven't you, O friend of mine,
This simple axiom found?

To be joyous with and by yourself,
Is the true path to happiness?

19.
No Sounds Are Ever So Nice And True

No sounds are ever so nice and true,
As are the whispers of a rolling river,
And who was ever wealthier than
The one who of his heart is a giver?

Cos the givers of wealth,
Take time to accumulate it,
And longer still,
For their hearts to be lit,

And only an enlightened heart,
Does the darkness in another's see,
And it has but nothing else to give,
For nothing else is free.

Isn't it strange then, O Ashok,
How miserly we can be,
To give of our time and ourselves to others,
When that is all we have to give, seemingly!

20.
Bury Me If You Will

Bury me if you will,
But the truth will never die,
And who was ever remembered,
For a spoken lie?

Stars will come and stars will go,
Never mind how high,
But who will ever bet, tell me,
Against an eternal sky?

Sleight of hand is a bit of magic,
As is the smooth and glib tongue,
But apples have you ever seen
From a banana tree, hung.

So what if anything does this say
Of duplicity and the world,
Where barbs in the guise of roses sweet,
Are oft at the innocents hurled,

That there is in all of us,
Both innocence and design,
And we can never with certainty
The human mind define.

21.
I Sing, I Pray

I sing, I pray,
For two meals a day,
Will someone help
Will someone pay?

Or will you just pass me by,
Hide your face and walk away,
For that is what I mostly see,
Mostly guilt, no sympathy,

Did you your parents wilfully choose?
Or was it destiny?
That you were born to affluence,
To rule and lord over me?

What if I were king and you the subject?
Then you'd be begging just like me.
So isn't it just a matter of chance,
That some won't walk while other's will dance?

And that is what we call destiny,
To rebel against but to no avail,
To resign to cruel fate,
Or,
With wisdom accept and happily too,
That what destiny unfolds is, alas, true.

22.
Go Light A Lamp In Another's Heart

Go light a lamp in another's heart,
And that flame will never die,
Cos someone will always have,
Something to remember you by.

There is no greater brilliance,
Than the radiance of a smile,
When a heart is all lit up,
It will radiate many a mile.

No star is ever so bright,
As the sparkle in the eye,
When the lamp in a heart you light,
And that's the reason why.

And if that's not good enough reason,
I'll tell you another that's true,
When you light up another's heart,
You light up your own too.

23.
Carry A Basket Of Dreams

Carry a basket of dreams
From ennui to find relief,
Remember, the start of a journey,
Is no more than just belief.

Build a bridge of faith
On a pond of justice and truth,
And lead a life that's pure,
Sincere, not uncouth.

Like many an unsung hero,
Do all that which you have to,
For simply in the doing,
Are rewards lasting and true.

No sermons are ever needed,
For those who their heart and conscience heeded.

24.
Is There A Tavern In The Sky

Is there a tavern in the sky
And fountains spraying wine?
Is there magic beyond the clouds,
Are stars strung by vine?

So far removed from frailties,
Is that land called divine?
Where all belongs to the One above,
And nothing is called mine?

Is there any darkness there?
Is there a sun to shine?
Is there longing, is there want?
Do angels also pine?

If forgiveness for sin is true Ashok,
Then why is there a hell?
Will someone this conundrum answer,
Will someone please tell.

If there's redemption for the soul,
Then why were we made less than whole?

25.
Life's A Labyrinth, A Veritable Maze

Life's a labyrinth, a veritable maze,
Like the strings of stars at which we gaze,
Like a winter's day when it's foggy and cold,
And the day turns night midst mist and haze.

Like the freshness of spring when winter's done,
And the melting of snow has just begun,
Like rivulets coursing o'er pebble and dale,
And the orange glow of a setting sun.

It's magical, then it's up and down,
Tatters turn to resplendent gown,
A charming smile and before you know,
The forehead creased with an ugly frown,

So take the rough with the smooth,
In your stride and move on,
And soon enough will troubles end,
Like a visiting nightmare that's come and gone.

26.
Why Does The Sun Set?

Let's look at it philosophically,
Or romantically if you will,
Why does the sun daily set,
And darkness bring until

It meets another dawn some place,
To herald another day,
Is it to bring a lesson home?
Or, let romance have its say?

The sermon being to simply say,
Unspokenly and true,
That which glows and daily shines,
Will fade and vanish too,

Power, glory, beauty and fame,
Must learn and understand,
The brightness of day is ephemeral,
And Time no more than shifting sand,

But as the sun gives away to moon,
And the stars come shining bright,
Darkness does and always will,
Bring an end to daylight.

Enjoy your day, your light, your time,
But then, you need to sleep too,
And that is why the sun like all things wise,
Gently sets and bids adieu.

27.
The Mind That Is Not Buffeted By Winds

The mind that is not buffeted by winds
Is like the lamp that does not flicker,
Like the shore that does but storms weather,
Like the heart that feels for another,

Like the ship that has a working rudder,
Like the eyes of a doting mother,
For it does but look after you,
And shows the way that's righteous and true.

It keeps your skies bright and blue,
Away from clouds and rain too,
And like the sun that shines through
Fog and mist and blizzard too,

It takes care of you and does it well,
So, let the mind decide what is right,
Never let conscience out of sight,
Or else dark will replace gentle light,

Remember, might is never right,
The straight and narrow is always tight,
And to walk it is an eternal fight
Between that which is good and bad,
Things that keep you happy or sad,
It doesn't take an awful lot,
To keep you merry, keep you glad,

Be happy then with what you've got,
Cos more than that was not your lot,
Perhaps, it's destiny you forgot,

In your greed and envy then,
You use your power and your pen,
To multiply truth by the number ten,
And in the process you forget
And place your all on a losing bet,

But it is all a zero sum game,
If you look at the end of both name and fame,
So never another should you blame,
Cos no one's different
We're all the same,
Simply mortal, simply frail,
And that is all there is
To the human tale.

28.
Life’s An Amalgam Of Sunshine And Rain

Life’s an amalgam of sunshine and rain,
All pleasure laced with tinges of pain
Life is about happiness and good cheer,
And surely not about loss and gain.

So why should we from joy abstain,
And treat each moment like an onrushing train,
That we must catch or sidestep,
And thoughts of the worst in our minds entertain.

It's not mysterious, it's not arcane,
If balance of mind we try to maintain,
Those who lived and died before us,
Also had frost on their window pane.

But not all the time nor in the main
Was there cloud and incessant rain,
Silver linings always there,
So why should we worry about the strain?

Live it full without disdain,
Cos life is never ever a bane,
It's a gift, a blessing, it truly is,
And in the Lord's rightful domain.

29.
Like The Drooping, Wilting Hibiscus

Like the drooping, wilting hibiscus,
That's had its days of joy,
Does a grieving heart in smithereens lie,
Like a tiny broken toy.

The smile that once lit up the eyes,
No longer adorns the face,
The sun does a cloud find,
When happiness has run its race.

Bereft of light the moon above,
Whilst there, is never seen,
And birds that lose their love and more,
Don't strut, don't preen.

If a hibiscus could only cry, Ashok,
'Twould surely do when saying goodbye.

30.
Each One Has A Destiny

Each one has a destiny,
All written and ordained,
And while we must our deeds do,
The fruit may never be obtained,

For that is the governing principle,
Of all that bear a life,
And not a line can you erase,
Use pen, scythe or knife.

For as night makes way for day,
So does life for demise,
And those that this happily accept,
Stay content and are worldly-wise.

No greater wealth was ever known,
Than contentment when in hearts sown.

31.
What Was It Like In The Womb?

What was it like in the womb?
What will it be like in the tomb?
It's not morbid, it's not gory,
It's the start and the end of the human story.

And between the two does life reside,
And journey we do to complete the ride
Of days and nights and breaths of air,
As joys and tears and fears we share.

For that is all there is to it,
This world that is by the sun lit,
So make the most of moment each,
Then, the meaning of life is within reach.

32.
The Arsenals Of Military Might

The arsenals of military might,
Are they not visible signs?
Do they not suggest to us,
The failure of peace, hearts and minds?

Will they not like monsters be,
That turn upon their creators
And far from being great deterrents,
Will they not make us 'haters'?

And do they not willy-nilly,
Resources misallocate,
And deprive the starving millions,
Of food, and lives devastate?

So who but the makers benefit,
From these efforts to peace maintain?
While the ordinary man duly suffers
In silence, living a life of pain.

We live in a world of sham today
A jungle where might is right,
And no one cares for another,
Inherent goodness, out of sight.

The divide between man and man,
Never greater than now,
And armaments just reinforce,
The yawning gap, and how.

And Nature too its warnings gives,
To within us awaken,
The dormant seed of brotherhood and peace,
Or be ready for annihilation.

But isn't this all naive, Ashok,
For won't we soon be overrun?
By forces inimical to our interests,
If we're without a gun!!

33.
Disarmament Is Now A Forgotten Word

Disarmament is now a forgotten word,
In no one's lexicon,
Selective in its meaning,
Don't believe me, ask the UN.

I am 'nuclear' so you can't be,
You may be rogue and not good like me!
Logical sounding wouldn't you say,
In a world where you can't tell night from day?

If God created this messy world,
And an even messier man,
He will find a way out of this,
For only He surely can,

Cos we seem to be doing all we can,
To put an end to it,
O Wisdom, where art thou?
And in man why so dimly lit?

34.
My India

Thousands of years of history,
And a majesty all its own.
Has my India truly though,
Exponentially grown?

Six decades and more now,
Since the freedom that she won,
Non-violently and peacefully,
Without the aid of a gun.

Hopes and aspirations loom large,
For the building of a future,
As one people with a golden heritage,
Do their motherland nurture.

The clarion call of Independence,
United one and all,
But alas, and decades later,
Do we on unity stand tall?

Are we Indians first and last,
Is what I truly ask?
Are we free to move around,
And in the country bask?

Regardless of the place of birth,
Regardless of the speech,
Welcome as the locals are,
All with in easy reach.

Are there barriers on the way,
Linguistic and others?
That make us act and behave,
Not quite like loving brothers.

Have we built on the dreams,
Of those who fought and died,
For the cause of being yoke-free,
Would they have seen today and cried?

Where did we go wrong, I wonder,
And what should it have been?
What can we do to set things right,
To unite and lessen the din?

What can't be undone why cry over?
But lessons we can learn,
From which to reform and, perhaps,
New leaves of hope turn.

Unity demands a certain minimum,
Or else it's a laboured ask,
Diversity in every realm and sphere,
Makes it a difficult task.

Do we not need to speak to each other,
In a language we all understand?
How then do we achieve this,
Without a common language at hand?

No other case in history,
Has a people with so many tongues,
For all that does is simply test,
Minds and the power of lungs.

So, a national language we must have,
That all can happily speak,
In addition to the mother tongue,
And we'll reach the mountain peak.

Civilisations are grand and great,
But baggages they also carry,
And hence we see the EU,
Not able to truly marry.

Disparate as they are,
They are proud of their races,
The US does not the baggage carry,
Cos as a nation it's only walked a few paces.

So a working national lingo we surely need,
And Hindi was chosen as the seed,
But will it flower, will it bloom?
Or will the sky be tinged with gloom?

Surely English it must not be,
Cos from the English we were free
In '47, and since then we haven't yet found,
One language that does the round?

Are our gods multi-lingual, I wonder?
If we don't do something soon enough,
Will we be torn asunder,
I Wonder?

35.
The Sunset Years

A bit above the skyline now,
A fading orange glow,
No longer bright the setting sun,
Its paces getting slow.

Time takes its weary toll,
As evening shadows loom large,
And somewhere in the distance floats,
The waiting destined barge,

The Oarsman knows it best of all,
For it's in his boat we ride,
And when He does a calling come,
There is no place to hide.

Sunset time is reflection time,
As you look at the past in the eye,
And nothing but the truth do you see,
For mirrors never lie.

Sunset time must be contentment time,
However restless you may be,
A time to thank your Maker,
As you stare at eternity.

Life is but a rocking chessboard,
Kings and queens and pawns et al,
Tossed and turned at the Master's will,
All pieces designed to finally fall.

36.
When You Are With Dust Covered

When you are with dust covered
And meet the land of your birth
Will you then be fondly remembered?
For that alone is true worth.

Will someone have on their lips,
And in their hearts too,
Something nice to remember you by,
A kind word or two.

Will someone look up at the stars,
And there look for you,
And wonder where it all went,
And where and how time flew?

And peace will your soul beget,
When you look down from above,
And see someone look up for you,
With tears of warmth and love.

37.
Your Ego, Your Friend, Your Foe

Hold a mirror unto yourself,
Don't tell me what you see,
Is that really you, Ashok,
Or, is there more of me?

Mirrors do no more than reflect,
What faces them you see,
And I am one behind the scenes,
Working surreptitiously.

The mirror never gets to see me,
But you, for sure do,
Cos I am your Ego,
And always close to you.

I am good for you in measures small,
Good for your self-esteem,
But too much of me is just no good,
Cos you'll never wake from your dream.

Be careful then, be careful of me,
Cos if I get the upper hand,
I shall make you both
Fake and Ugly.

38.
When The Road Ends And The Goal Is Achieved

When the road ends and the goal is achieved,
Why then do I feel so aggrieved,
Lost and wayward once again,
Is that the destiny of all men
Who for ends and destinations look?
And so,
Miss reading Life's open book,
Where the journey is of nights and days,
Through alleys, paths and myriad ways.

Each a *manzil**, each an end,
A waiting sea at the river's bend,
Who knows what Time unfolds,
And who what the morrow holds?

The journey is all there is to life,
As traverse you do through joy and strife,
'Tis up to you to deal with it,
As you walk through Time, both dark and lit,

Towards the mountain and the abyss too,
Sure of self with doubts few,
Until!

Stages there are but destinations not?
And at the end nothing's the lot.

So, let's enjoy the journey, friends,
Without motives, without ends,
Roses with thorns in all gardens you'll find,
And destinations are but delusions of the mind.

**Manzil* in Urdu means destination

39.
Utopia Or Dystopia

Utopia or dystopia,
Take your chosen pick,
With reality by your side,
Imaginary cameras you can click.

All good and all bad,
We shall never find,
Cos bits of both exist,
In all mankind,

Ingrained in the psyche,
And the human DNA,
Complex are the rules we see,
Both at work and play.

Mostly moral is the norm,
Facetious as it may sound,
But a saint without sin,
Who has ever found?

For designed we are in manner such,
That to walk the straight and narrow,
In the billowing winds of tortured emotion,
Ain't easy for the human marrow.

So each step that you softly tread
Keep conscience by your side,
Tough it may be, friends, to do,
But surely, less tumultuous will be your ride.

40.
Drop By Drop Do Tears An Ocean Make

Drop by drop do tears an ocean make,
But the ocean does not my thirst slake,
For what I need, O heart of mine,
Is tranquillity and peace divine,

And not the turmoil of the seas,
No lashing winds but balmy breeze,
To take me 'cross the waters deep,
As I drift into gentle sleep,

Into the land of make-believe,
Where burdens I can shed and leave,
And dream of clouds and mountain tops,
And places where joy never stops,

Where laughter does the air fill,
And tears roll down my cheeks until,
It's time to bid the night goodbye,
As dawn lights up the waiting sky,

And the ocean of my spent tears,
With one last sigh, runs dry.

41.
If I Were A Desert Storm

If I were a desert storm,
I'd raze them all to the ground,
No place then for worldly worship,
Would ever again be found.

When God lives in the hearts of Man,
Why do we brick and mortar need?
For Truth is there in all of us,
If only we'd pay it heed.

Ironic that at an altar we pray,
Then forget what holy books say,
Merrily go about our daily chores,
And values with disdain, slay.

But if instead, your heart was the temple
No effort would you have to make,
To travel where you could kneel and pray,
And your blessings with you take.

So think, O friends, and pray if you will,
To the God that resides within you,
Go if you must to Man's structures,
But don't forget what is True.

42.
Winters Take Their Normal Toll

Winters take their normal toll,
On me and my flowers too,
The brilliant reds and radiant greens,
Now downcast and feeling blue.

The trees that were verdant with leaves,
Now barren logs of wood,
Home to no one amongst the birds,
Not even those with a hood.

The sun's trajectory lower now,
Its glow and warmth now timid,
A strange feebleness, no majesty there,
In what once was bright and pellucid.

And a yearning now for the slopes no more,
No ice, no snows for me,
O where are you, O searing summer?
Cos I would rather scalded be.

43.
All Is Fair In Love And War

All is fair in love and war,
And at the altar of expediency,
What you need to do you need to do,
And in the world of today,
That is shockingly true.

When it's all about power and pelf,
And the dollar is all supreme,
Every currency is at its mercy,
And the greenback is all you see.

Who cares about democracy
Or the welfare of the people?
I come first and last too,
For that is all that matters,
Others can take a running jump,
Or simply lie in tatters,

So hypocritical is 'sympathy',
I wonder if the word can be spelled,
I wonder how long before Man is
By his own follies felled?

44.
Man Created God Did You Say?

Man created God did you say?
Perhaps he did, in a certain way,
But it was all for the common good,
Cos he then had someone
to whom he could pray,
Or else he would have
been just victim to
The power of the moment,
The God of the day.

And if he did in his wisdom
Create the Almighty and if that is true,
And from that source sustenance find,
Some strength, some peace of mind,
Pray, tell me,
What wrong did he do?
For he only saw the warring crowd,
Man against man, abrasive and loud,
While he for peace did eagerly long,
And so created the psalm, the song.

The word today is 'democracy',
Rule of brute majority,
And so it is with believers today,
They outnumber the rest, they do,
And by a long way.

So who came first
The chicken or the egg?
Does it matter?

Even if Man created his Lord,
He did so with vision, clear and broad,
And look at the vastness of it all,
The all-encompassing, all-knowing bit,
Omniscient, omnipresent, omnipotent,
For man to look up to,
At the stars and the skies blue, at God.
And through that realise,
What is false and what true.

Ingenious,
If out of imagination He grew.
And if God created Man,
Then where is the fuss?
So think,
Either way, Man wins.

So what does the non-believer achieve,
By denying His presence,
Does he not grieve?
And when he does whose shoulder does he cry on,
When no one has the time
With camaraderie gone?
And so,

To the hapless non-believer, I say,
Find yourself a better way,
To help you through stressful times,
Than having to rely on just yourself,
With your limited knowledge and little power,
Or else your solace will be just nursery rhymes.

45.
The Old Sock

The old sock,
And the old shoe,
Give us great comfort,
Isn't that true?

Neither holes nor anything else,
Nothing matters,
Does happiness lie I often wonder,
In rags and tatters?

And so it is
With values old,
They don't tarnish
As does not gold.

There's a lot to say for old morality,
Changing mores notwithstanding,
Battles rage and will rage on,
Let's see who'll be the last man standing.

46.
One Swallow Does Not A Summer Make

One swallow does not a summer make,
Nor a single star the sky,
A million lies never a truth,
And contentment is never a sigh.

All that glitters isn't gold,
All stars don't always shine,
Wings will not man a bird make,
Nor sainthood make him divine.

There's more than meets our eyes too,
Invisible, as is the Lord,
Evil we can never see,
Nor the goodness in a broad.

There is no smoke without a fire,
No storm without a warning,
There must cloud be for rain,
And dawn to break for the morning.

Birds of a feather flock together,
And so it is with us,
Colour, caste, creed and tongue,
The cause of all the fuss!

Ifs and buts, do's and don'ts,
All have their rightful place,
Ups and downs, joy and grief,
Are all part of Life's race.

47.
You've Got It All Wrong

You've got it all wrong, O, Man of today,
For Belief is not meant to be analysed,
A prayer is not to seek nor ask,
Nor is it to be rationalised.

An honest prayer is not for reward,
Nor to success seek or find,
If anything it is a *tête-à-tête*
With oneself, for peace of mind.

Just think:

If eight billion people pray with a cause
Other than peace of mind,
The good Lord would have a helluva task,
To everyday the time find
To give you a job, a car and a wife,
And, perhaps, me another life.

We pray for rain and ease of pain,
And pray for favours plain,
We pray for health and also wealth,
And do so with skilful stealth,
With eyes shut and folded hands,
So no one knows nor understands,
What's in the mind nor in the heart,
Just so that a wish gets a head start.

Belief must just belief be,
No more, no less, at least for me.

48.
It's That Time Of The Year

It's that time of the year
When the sun goes down,
A lot sooner now,
It seems in my town.

Its trajectory's lower,
It seems nearer to me,
But that doesn't matter,
Cos it's winter you see.

I see snow clad mountains,
And it's cold outside,
Remember, nearness doesn't always,
Bring warmth to your side.

The trees bereft of leaves,
No nightingale there to sing,
Desolate, bare and wanting,
The sun to warmth bring.

But all bleak it isn't,
Cos there's a freshness in the air,
The spring in my step tells me.
It's time for winter wear.

So out come the woollies
Caps, scarves and mittens blue,
For the chill of winter is well known,
And I know it too.

Time to ski down slopes,
If that is your fancy,
Or a book to read by the fire,
A le Carré or a Clancy.

And when the sun's day is done
It does seem too soon,
To look up at the sky,
In search of the missing moon.

So a snooze by the fire,
Would in order be,
Until the eyes begin to droop,
And it's sleep time for me.

49.
Retribution

No matter how much we might have changed,
We still have to pay for misdeeds a price,
That is the law of retribution, friends,
That is fair, but may not be nice.

An eye for an eye and a tooth for a tooth,
Does seem a little harsh I know,
Cos what happens then to forgiveness and mercy?
And for that where does one then go?

No clear answers emerge unless,
We believe it's all here on Earth,
Heaven and hell and all in between,
From the time that we take birth.

Would make us more responsible wouldn't it?
If we believed in this philosophy,
We would have to take the blame for actions,
And not shift it to destiny.

And therein lies the rub I'm afraid,
The dichotomy for you and me.

50.
Just Be Yourself

When next you look at a mirror Ashok,
The mirror will perforce ask,
If it's not you that it really sees,
Why are you wearing a mask?

For the mirror knows and so do you,
And so does your 'seeing' heart,
You can do what you like to be someone else,
But a fake is a fake from the start.

You may wax eloquent all you like,
And speak with the mirror what you will,
But your eyes will reveal the truth to you,
Before a mirror when you stand still.

Why is it tough to be yourself,
When that is all you are?
Why would you want to tarnish it,
Why an honest face mar?

51.
Random Thoughts

If you wish to see
The sunny side of me,
Show me no frowns
And crease-free be,
There's a beginning and an end,
To all life, my friend,
What happens in between
Is the real mystery.

No one owes you anything,
No one owes you cheer,
To keep yourself happy,
Is your responsibility,

And if the spirit of despair,
Does descend on you,
Look up at the sky,
And set yourself free,

For despair is no more
Than a temporary dark cloud,
That hangs over your head
Then clears gradually.

The most profound thoughts and words,
Are both very simple and simply true,
There is no greater power than Truth.
And lies by their nature uncouth too.

And if the tongue doesn't slip,
And doesn't give you away,
The eyes will always, remember,
The truth say.

The mirror only tells you
How pretty you are,
Cos true beauty, my dear,
Lies in the heart's bower.

And time is of the essence for all living things,
And Time is patience and that happiness brings,
People don't hum with crows remember,
Everyone hums when only the nightingale sings,

So bring a smile to your face,
When your heart lies heavy,
And even if it's forced
'Twill take care of most things.

52.
I Look At The Ocean Then At Myself

I look at the ocean then at myself,
And how small I seem to be,
Like the tiny star that I see in the distance,
Looking down at the smallness of me.

I'm not even a drop in the mighty ocean,
Nor would a million like me make,
The tiniest of waves that hit the shore,
And grains of sand like me, take.

The majesty of one and the frailty of the other,
How stark the contrast that I see,
The vastness of the waters, the endless horizon,
And the puny little six foot me.

Nature, O Nature, you are supreme,
And I, like a leaf, destined to fall,
No more am I than a fading dream,
That is always beyond recall.

53.
Leaves On My Tree

Two yellow and a thousand green,
Leaves on my tree, that's my scene,
But why the yellow, isn't that unfair?
Why does the tree have to be so mean?

Just cos they're old is that reason enough,
To make them less verdant, isn't the tree rough?
Why do these questions come to my mind?
The answers aren't easy, they are tough.

But why do I need to defend the leaves,
Cos there's always a beginning as well as an end,
And that's true for all that breathe naturally,
Cos Time is the master and all will bend.

The answer lies just in the passage of Time,
So why look for reason and why rhyme?
Enjoy every moment, every bit,
For once in the grave there'll be no lamp lit.

Colours and wrinkles come with age,
But don't put joy in a mental cage,
Turn over the leaves that don't read well,
Remember, life and laughter are on the same page.

54.
My Dreams

I can't fly but soar I can,
When to my thoughts wings I give,
And grounded though I well may be,
In many places do I live.

For all I do is visualise
Just where I want to be,
Transport myself via Time and Space.
Then let my eyes just see.

The world is thus at my feet,
Mountain, desert, dale and moor,
Oceans I can sail at will,
And return, when I choose, to shore.

Some dreams do I thus realise,
Those that daylight may not see,
So mingle with the clouds I do, and
Succumb to pleasure and fancy.

My mind is like the soaring eagle,
That measures the skies to and fro,
Swoops down from heights to plumb the depths,
And get ready again to go.

So join me on my travels, will you?
And make dreams come true.

55.
My 'Spiritual' Days

My 'spiritual' days are over,
Don't tempt me with that malt,
With the grape I'll be in clover,
Or else, 'twill be your fault.

I loved the *Lagavulin*,
Cos it wasn't *Black and White*,
And it never did me ruin,
Drinking through the night.

And with the colours of the label,
Red, green, black and blue,
'Twas fun with Aesop's Fable,
Cos the stories seemed true.

But what really brought down the house,
Was my fondness for the *Talisker*?
Sammy, my pal, always had a *Grouse*,
Why was I in with *Old Smuggler*?

There's a time and place for all things,
And that gives fun and joy,
But when a crow not a nightingale sings,
It's time to say, "O Boy".

56.
Keep Alight The Fire

If all the dreams I ever dreamt,
Were, one day, to come true,
Life would seem meaningless, wouldn't it?
Wouldn't you agree, wouldn't you?

The cup of joy must never run dry,
Nor must the cup in the tavern,
Don't ask me why this must be,
Cos it's finally ashes in urn.

So it's all about keeping hope alive,
For if that were ever to die,
You'd be constantly looking skywards,
No gleam, no glint in the eye.

There's a need to keep alight the fire,
A dream, a wish, some desire.

57.
The Reaper

The scythe with which you cut the rye,
Is that the scythe in the Reaper's hand?
Will you be prostrate when he strikes?
Or be taken as you stand?

Who knows what the morrow holds?
As the Sun turns night into day,
Will there another dawn be?
Who knows what there is to say?

What is real is the here and now
Icy winds or sweat on the brow,
When of a breath you aren't sure,
What more can you say, what more?

For the Reaper is a patient being
So keep him waiting till you're ready,
You'll know when your time is up,
When all around is unsteady.

58.
A Smile Is Like A Million Rays

Winds will blow and rivers don't rest,
The rains will rainbows carry,
Destiny's there to hold your hand,
So keep walking, why tarry?

We feel let down, often we do,
By those who walk beside us,
But forgiveness lies within our hearts,
And that is always a big plus.

Immortal is he, who mortality accepts,
Then weighs both deeds and words,
And when the going gets unduly tough
His loins he firmly girds.

Solace you'll find in the aftermath,
Of both hurricane and 'quake,
And nothing, but nothing ever,
Should the pillars of faith shake.

Winter does a lesson teach
On how to beat the chill,
Warmth you need against both
Inclement weather and ill-will.

Greatness lies in simplicity
And that is just being yourself,
It has little to do with name and fame,
And nothing with power and pelf.

A smile is like a million rays
Of the sun that shines above,
And blessed is he who understands
The power and warmth of love.

59.
My Mirror

Tell me mirror who am I
For I now see a different me?
Who is fake and who real?
The one I knew or the one I now see?

Do you find me like you did,
Or do I a stranger seem?
Is it dawn or twilight time?
Am I awake or in a dream?

Do you the honest truth reflect?
Or are you less than honest too?
Do you like me too pretend?
And not show me who I am, who?

Not all mirrors, like all men,
Do always tell the truth, as is.
Are you honest with me, tell me,
Or is flattery your daily biz?

What If I never looked at you,
Would it make me a better me?
Shorn of props for the ego
Would I better person be?

What then would you do, O mirror,
If no one ever looked at you?
To keep you in existence then,
I promise I'll look at you, I do.

60.
The Voice Of The Times

The voice of the times,
May not always be right,
But you still have to listen,
So as not to lose sight

Of things that are changing,
And moods that prevail,
Or else you'll be left standing
Like a ship without sail,

To be rocked by the winds,
And buffeted by storms,
Cos you're out of sync
With values and norms.

All things evolve,
Even rights and wrongs,
The melody of life,
Its tunes and its songs,

So go with the times, you must always do,
Even if it's tough, Ashok, for you.

61.
Why Does The Sun Play Hide And Seek

O, why does the sun play hide and seek,
And leave me to the winter's chill?
I wish these trees had no leaves,
Until…

'Twas time again for mellow spring,
When mountainsides are not snow clad,
Butterflies flit from flower to flower,
And my heart tells me it's feeling glad.

Snow and skies and slopes as well,
The cold was once fun for me,
Not any more is it now,
And some, I know, will surely agree.

There's a time and place for things all,
And the wise know when to bend, when to stand tall.

62.
Ordinary Man

I am an ordinary man like no other,
But ordinary we all are,
Your mirror will tell you how ordinary,
So you don't have to go very far.

Two lips and a nose and two brown eyes,
A forehead and a dimpled chin,
A shock of hair on a balding head,
Some 'ordinaries' are heavy, some thin.

That's all that my mirror shows,
So the rest of the ordinary me,
Can't be much to write home about,
Perhaps, less than ordinary.

And just before you begin to feel,
A sense of swelling pride,
Let me tell you, my dear reader,
Your mirror has to you lied,

Cos you too are pretty ordinary,
And an awful lot like me,
And I hope you will not angry get,
When the truth you begin to see,
For we're all quite
O R D I N A R Y.

63.
Silver Sun

A silver sun is what I saw today,
Through mist, haze and cloud,
Its usual brilliant, dazzling self,
Muted and much less proud.

And as I looked it in the eye,
It seemed to humbly say,
"Tell me little earthly stranger,
Do you like my silver ray?"

It seemed to me to be twilight time,
Though dawn it was, I know,
The glow was more of the moon,
And the sun a pale shadow.

O what has Man done to you,
You golden orb in the sky?
Robbed you of your magnificence,
Made all of Nature cry.

Protect the environment is what we merrily say,
Then go about our business, polluting all the way.

64.
Lead Your Life

Lead your life and lead it well,
For no other can you lead,
And every word that you speak,
Must match your every deed.

All is action cos everything moves,
And nothing is static ever,
Until with your last breath you do
Your ties for ever sever.

We're all one with the Cosmos,
The stars, the sun and the moon,
The world is one and shall always be,
And that is but Life's tune.

Good morning, good night and then a goodbye,
A laugh, a tear and then a sigh,
All this and more is destiny,
Until the day we quietly lie.

65.
Remove The Cobwebs From Your Mind

In one hand do I a lamp hold,
In the other the pursuing shadow,
To remind myself that nothing lasts,
Nor is there an eternal glow,

For that which daily shines,
Does also make way for night,
And those that brightly see today,
May one day lose sight.

And that which moves but constantly,
Will someday lie so still,
You'll never know how quiet life is,
You'll never know, until,

But pre-empt you can and in quiet live,
And peace in living find,
If once in a while, but every day,
You empty out your mind.

For in the clean-up you will for ever
Cobwebs from the mind remove,
And leave yourself with happier tunes,
And in much better groove.

66.
Time Does Run Out For All

Time does run out for all,
In the hourglass for each,
And every grain of sand that falls,
A diminishing lesson does teach.

Nights and days are far too vague,
Says that little grain of sand,
I am the moment remember,
Your destiny in my hand.

And as I gently pass through
Your past closeted within me,
The next grain is yours to fill,
With present memory.

That is all there is to life,
Just grains of sand in the glass,
And, O how soon they drop!
How soon do they pass!

67.
The Passage Of Time

Drawing lines in the sand,
Mimicking those of the hand,
Lines that vanish with the passage of time,
Aren't words lovely when in rhyme?

Much like what friendship is,
When harmony does warmth bring,
Unlike the harshness of winter's chill,
Heart-warming, the footsteps of impending Spring.

Then summer does its toll take,
And autumn a riot of colour make,
As trees ready to shed their leaves,
In gentle and in balmy breeze.

The green of the hills hidden by mist,
And mountain tops all sun-kissed,
The first signs of snow around,
On the peaks to be now found.

The circle thus complete,
Nature's designs are hard to beat.

68.
O How Faint The Memory Now

O how faint the memory now,
Of those I loved and lost,
Time's the healer, it surely is,
But erasure is the cost.

Like mist and fog that hide the sun,
Behind their veil and cloud,
Memories too are entombed,
And blanketed by Time's shroud.

But thank the Lord, O Ashok,
Or else 'twould impossible be,
To live a life of relative peace,
And from constant grief, free.

Forgetfulness then is necessary friends,
And so too the fading memory,
That blurs the past to let us live,
And do so but happily.

69.
Contrariness

Weeds in the green, like pebbles in the stream,
And nightmares as you sleep,
Upsetting your dream,
How quiet the shore, O, tell me no more,

For I know there are storms,
In the oceans, galore,
The good and the bad,
Are in each one of us,

Go ride a ship, take a bus.
And what would be good if there wasn't a bad?
And happiness what,
If you never were sad?

Heaven and hell are both within,
As is piety and also sin.

70.
O Night, I Do But Long For Thee

O Night, I do but long for thee
From the first colours of morn,
When chirping sparrows awaken me,
To herald the break of dawn.

For this dreamless day that I foresee,
Of men and machines galore,
Bereft of all tranquillity,
And everyone after more.

More of this and more of that,
For nothing ever seems enough,
Desire, greed, envy and show,
Just piling up of stuff.

But in your arms, O night, I do
Sleep and dream perchance,
And with fairies that glide by me,
I often get to dance.

So night over day scores for me,
And sleep over waking hours,
Tell me, someone, what in the day
Is ever prettier than stars?

71.
No Dark Was Ever So Dark

No dark was ever so dark friend,
No darkness that will never end,
No night was ever, ever so long,
No wail that will not break into song.

No hope that will light not see,
No bondage that will not get free,
Nothing that can the spirit contain,
No heights that you cannot attain.

If faith you have in yourself,
No power or any kind of pelf,
Can hold you down and keep you there,
For we're all subject to wear and tear.

There is a time for each of us,
Whoever said there's an eternal bus,
Each moment that we then spend well,
Has its own little story to nicely tell,

So wallow not in despair ever,
Not until from life you sever,
All connection,
For then it will but matter not,
What was your human lot.

72.
Winding Road

Winding road and winding ways,
Nothing's straight out there today,
Double entendre, tweets and twerps,
People don't mean what they say.

Mirrors don't tell the face a fact,
Reflection no longer is pause and think,
Equilibrium is a foreign word,
Cos it's either rise or simply sink.

But don't worry, be happy,
For it's your life that you lead,
Like it's my right to write,
And yours to read or not read.

You can't live as others want,
Nor would you wish to do that,
So why comment on their style,
Let's just leave it at that.

73.
Illusive Dreams

Illusive as dreams are,
Do they a story tell?
A sign give, a mark leave,
And often ring a bell?

Does the night reveal more,
And daylight secrets keep,
Is that why the future unfolds,
While, unmindfully, we sleep?

Do we the conscience put on hold,
As long as we stay awake?
For us to do our dirty chores,
For us to greed, slake?

Does darkness within itself contain
The very light it hides?
Saints are sinners and vice versa,
Why take sides?

Let's wish for dreams and dreams alone,
But if it's nightmares, please don't moan,
For they too a message bring,
You're barking too much.
So try to sing.

74.
Strange Are Your Ways

Strange are your ways, O Lord
Inexplicable,
But why do I have to understand how you work,
For faith and belief are beyond scrutiny,
Or should be,
Else 'twould be blasphemy,
Wouldn't it?

And when I give you form and shape,
Statues of you do I make,
To re-enforce this faith of mine,
I do so for my own sake,
For I can then converse with you.

Pray and look into your eyes,
As I do with friends of mine,
And not just stare at the skies,
For you indeed are my friend,
The one to whom I kneel and bend,
True and honest with you, O Lord,
For with you why would I pretend?

Cos there's nothing that you do not know,
Nothing that I need to show
Or hide,
Truth and nothing but the truth,
And with you I have never shied
Away from it.

You are always by my side,
And to you I am eternally tied,
The bond with you set in stone,
And for my sins I do atone,
Cos forgive I know you always will,
Until,
The day I merge with you.

75.
Patience

Patient beings will breast the tape
Ahead of impatient souls,
Cos they wait for smouldering embers to die,
And not haul themselves over coals.

Battered shores a story tell
Of storms, typhoons and din,
And yet, it is the shores, over time,
That patiently and calmly will win.

Rivers flow and endlessly,
Journeying to the sea,
No rock, no reef, no mountain ever,
Hindered their destiny.

There is virtue then in the waiting game,
To let things drop into place,
Cos slow and steady we know well,
Eventually wins the race.

76.
O, Silly Man

Wander we do through hill and dale,
And gaze at the distant sky,
Then daily pass by the self
Without thought, I wonder why?

How little of ourselves we know
And how little we really care,
Of the wonder that we all are,
When at the stars, bewildered, we stare.

No greater wonder than Man himself,
In all of Nature is there,
If only Man for greed and want,
Didn't himself ensnare.

Sit back and think, O silly Man,
Why must you another fight?
And through the darkness that clouds the mind
Will penetrate a revealing light.

Mortal as we all are,
We are immortal too,
For words and deeds we leave behind,
Are sometimes all too few.

77.
Beyond The Purlieus Of The Mind

Beyond the purlieus of the mind,
Beyond the stars what is there?
Consciousness is but minuscule,
And ignorance is everywhere.

Life is measured in terms of Time,
And Time in terms of years,
When you carry with you your history,
You carry with you your fears.

Here and now is all it is,
For the morrow's a pack of lies,
Predictions no more than wishes just,
Like dreamy, starry eyes.

But enjoy today with the sun you have,
Why worry about tomorrow's cloud,
So do what pleases you the most,
And ignore the motley crowd.

78.
Dew On The Leaves

I love the dew on the leaves,
And the heart that seldom grieves,
For it knows better than most,
And reality better perceives.

And Hope, that eternal friend,
Lifts the spirit and will not bend,
Until we live through joy and strife,
Until the very, very end.

For there is an order to all things,
That Nature in its wisdom brings,
Like trees that give us air to breathe,
And the nightingale that melody sings.

The colour green and the colour blue,
No other quite so soothing and true,
The brown of the earth home to all,
The dust on which we all grew.

All else is but a pack of lies,
Nothing hidden from seeing eyes,
No greater pathos ever expressed,
Than the lament in heartfelt sighs.

How I wish I knew this poem's end,
So leave it to you, my dear friend.

79.
Time The Master

Moments well-spent are truly eternal,
Cos they live in our hearts for ever,
To be fondly nurtured and always cherished,
To be severed but never.

Time's like the bird that wings away,
Never to return to base,
Your moment too is here and now,
The one that you just face.

Live it full and brim-fully
Cos another may not be yours,
So take a bow and thankfully,
For who knows about encores.

Twinkle time is time to sleep
And for stars to come out and play,
Do what you will or how you wish,
Time is the master all the way.

80.
An Ode To Summer

O summer, you are the anodyne,
For the woes of winter's freeze,
When the mind goes numb and the body chills,
And trees yearn for their leaves.

When all is stark, denuded and bare,
Or clad in frost and snow,
And the sun, when there, of little use,
Shorn of warmth and glow.

There's purity I concede,
In the whiteness of things,
And in the beauty that winter brings,
But I'd rather see these
On canvas if you please,
In the arms of summer with ease.

The first signs I see of you, O summer,
Have warmed my heart no end,
Of the seasons all, that Nature reveals,
You, my dear, are my best friend.

81.
The Road To Nowhere

The road to nowhere,
May well be the road for you,
When you've reached your destination,
And have nothing left to rue.

Remember the door swings both ways,
You can either go in or out,
And the tree that gives you shade,
May sometimes the sun cut out.

And tears have duality too,
To give relief and sympathy,
And there's always another view,
You may not always be right, you see.

And there's much to learn from another,
For no one knows it all,
And the mountain top you climb,
Is the one from which you fall.

Restraint wins over exuberance,
Be careful with what you say,
What escapes your lips, dear friends,
Are words that fly away.

Each night is the end of the day,
And dawn the start of another,
And so the chain of the past and the future,
Is but closely linked together.

82.
Being Alive Is Divine

Don't need to part the waters,
The way around is fine,
Don't need to prove a thing,
Just being alive is divine.

Each breath is life itself,
Each moment I live is mine,
That's all there is to it,
That is the grand design.

What is yours you'll surely get,
And that surely is fine,
For there's nothing beyond Destiny,
So why rave and rant, and pine?

Keep Hope alive in the heart,
And for that, faith is a good place to start.

83.
The River Of No Return

Life is but a river,
That ferries you to the sea,
Through rock and crag and meadows wide.
Into the arms of Eternity,

Gently aided by the zephyr,
Or buffeted by a storm,
And lest we forget we must remember,
In the cold we must keep warm.

And, the woollies of warmth are love and care,
And these you must always carry,
Then spread them wide and generously,
And in this you must not tarry.

Enjoy then this one-way ride,
For there's no going back to the past,
And every mile that you traverse,
May well be the very last.

84.
Remit The Anger

Remit the anger
Quell the storm
And feel the peace within,
The deepest part
Of you, will then
Be free of noise and din.

For anger does
But wisdom cloud
So the truth you don't see,
While inside of you
A little voice says,
"You're only hurting me".

There is no gain
In the anger game
And the only loser is you,
Why hurt yourself
Why masochist be
For every word here is true.

So be kind to self
Don't unkind be
To the one who matters most,
Life's a party of one
And no one but you
Is both guest and also host.

85.
Clues Of The Future Lie In The Seeds Of The Past

Clues of the future lie in the seeds of the past,
Slow down, O Man, cos you're going too fast,
Night follows day and you can't change that,
And you'll one day retire, however you bat.

Blue skies and the sun will come your way,
But you can't keep cloud and thunder at bay,
They too have a role to play we know,
Parched lands need rain, else where would you go?

Only one thing is certain, the end of life,
Cos you don't pay taxes if you live in Dubai,
Now that you know where the pot of gold is,
Go work with the Arabs and have fun in Hawaii.

ND - #0257 - 080726 - C0 - 197/132/9 - PB - 9781784560119 - Gloss Lamination